Postcards From The Hedge

Wishing I Was There?

First published 2020 by The Hedgehog Poetry Press

Published in the UK by
The Hedgehog Poetry Press
5, Coppack House
Churchill Avenue
Clevedon
BS21 6QW

www.hedgehogpress.co.uk

ISBN: 978-1-913499-58-7

Copyright © Mark Davidson 2020

The right of Mark Davidson to be identified as the editor of this work has been asserted in accordance with the Copyright, Designs and Patents Act 1988. All rights for individual works retained by the respective author.

All rights reserved. No part of this publication may be reproduced, stored in or introduced into a retrieval system, or transmitted in any form, or by any means (electronic, mechanical, photocopying, recording or otherwise) without prior written permissions of the publisher. Any person who does any unauthorised act in relation to this publication may be liable for criminal prosecution and civil claims for damages,

9 8 7 6 5 4 3 2 1

A CIP Catalogue record for this book is available from the British Library.

Poetry From...

John Priestley 5
Annie Maclean 6
Ceinwen E Cariad Haydon 7
Romina van Maaren 8
Darren J Beaney 9
Nigel Kent 10
Jane Avery 11
Margaret Royall 12
Sadie Maskery 14
David Mark Williams 15

JOHN PRIESTLEY

Postcard

I have basked in a sand-blasted deckchair
built a crenellated castle on golden sands
sucked pink lettered rock, dribbled a ninety-nine
seen the spangled dancers at the end of the pier
with their candy floss hair and glittery tights
bounced on a donkey, heard the tide-and-tide bell
toll the ebb and the flow, worn a kiss-me-quick hat
under the pier smelt the tang of salt
on the incoming breeze, seen the setting sun
slide into the sea eaten fish and chips
on the promenade picked sand from a sandwich
and gritted my teeth on the dodgems and rides
at the funfair down the beach and blinked in the darkness
of "Artificial Sunshine" and yet without illumination

I've not found where to go,
what to say, what to do,
to find you
         the answer.

ANNIE MACLEAN

Covidland

Summer 2020

An empty beach!

So much sand   [picture of a wave breaking on a sandy beach]
The shining sun.
The sparkling ocean.

        We're socially distanced from each other.
        Will we laugh at this when this is over?

[picture of a seagull]   The seagulls swoop.
        They're unaware of any virus.
        We send you love -
        so you won't forget us!

    Wish You Were Here!
    Much love,

CEINWEN E CARIAD HAYDON

thankful

interned
landlocked for months
denied breaths of sea air
readied for joy when freedom came
rebirth

thinking
of those we lost
stings sharper than salt winds
how should we honour their worth
with truth

ROMINA VAN MAAREN

Dear Louise,

This Summer, I'll dream.
I sail without a raft
and fly without wings.
No problem.
While sadness stays in me
The wind in my head
will take me where; the
thoughts in my mind
might wander away.
No worries.
While cares run up
There's books to read
and fish to eat, my bed
a beautiful island and
motion pictures to rescue.
No pleasure,
no nothing it is.
The world on fire, seasons
like never before. As soon as
the night sky shows her
twinkling street lights, only
then calmness rises down.
This Summer, I'll dream and
I'll pray. My bed an island,
my refuge. In Paradise:
Peaceful happyness,
Logical fearness.

Yours,
R.

DARREN J BEANEY

Picture postcard

You promenade beside the ocean. I balance
 on a barnacled breakwater, view a perfect
    picture postcard   -   you   sauntering across the beach.
    You walk my way.   I want to be the warming sun
tenderly beating down on your bronzed bare shoulders.
     I imagine myself as the nonchalant breeze
blowing like a satisfied sigh on your blushed cheek.
        I wish to be soft hot sand that feels so homely
under your feet. And I long to be the millions
   of tiny grains between your toes
         that you cannot help but take home.

NIGEL KENT

Shifting Sands

Fifty weeks of fifties,
crammed in an old jam jar;
he promised her a week
living like Jay Gatsby
on the southern coast of France,
but Lockdown grounded
all her winter-warming fantasies
of walking hand-in-hand
on sun-bathed beaches;
of dancing barefoot in his arms
to the silky rhythms of the waves.
No choice but a DIY
holiday at home, instead,
with a ton of builders' sand
raked across the yard;
and Mediterranean-blue emulsion
sloshed across the fence,
where they doze
for seven days in deckchairs,
dug from the back of the shed,
and sip consolation cocktails
they name Captain Tom
and the Furlough Funster,
as they empty plastic jugs of each,
and in her daytime dreams,
dressed like Jay and Daisy,
they build sunset castles
on the Riviera beach,
laughing uncontrollably
because the sand's too dry to shape,
oblivious to the storm clouds
gathering in the east.

JANE AVERY

Magic

A brimful of gappy grins
vying for a window seat
delight directing gangly limbs
a brimful of gappy grins.

The dunes call for Bedouins
the sea now glimpsed – bedlam begins
a brimful of gappy grins
vying for a window seat.

MARGARET ROYALL

A Postcard From Scarborough

Our old car scarcely made it
there and back, its engine
mostly cranked on hope
and fingers crossed.

Our destination Scarborough
in the 50s, about as far as
our faithful Austin 7 would go
without a mechanic on hand!

We always stayed at Mrs Gill's,
a modest boarding house
close to the sandy bay, where
pleasure boats winked sleepily

from the harbour wall. Their
owners vied to fill the decks
with trippers, a few sparse weeks
to glean their modest income.

A cruise around the bay, then
fish and chips out of newspaper -
always the first thing on our list, though
dive-bombing seagulls often spoiled the fun.

I think I was probably five years old
that time I got locked in the loo
at our B&B. Such utter panic!
It still lives on in my memory even now...

Mum tried to keep me calm with
clear instructions whispered through
the keyhole, until the stiff key finally
yielded to my trembling, tear-stained hands.

We would ride the scenic railway, take the
bus to Peasholm Park, hire a rowing boat
on the lake or have a go on the putting green.
For me it was a dreamland with Japanese shrubs,

statues and pagodas. I could be Alice
in Wonderland or Ratty in Wind in the
Willows; a myriad possibilities each day,
my young imagination running riot.

The fun-packed week flew by, savouring
each day minute by joyful minute, sad when
our time was up and normality called us home,
suitcases crammed with memories until the next time..

SADIE MASKERY

Postcard

Hello darling, hope you're well
I'm in Spain. I had a spell of
existential mum malaise
(perdí la cabeza) so
have buggered off on holidays
to find myself a Spanish beau
I mean a fit senor I think.
Not the guys all fat and smeggy
that you pull in sunny Skeggy.
I might have had a little drink.
Cuz oh my dear, not gonna lie,
I'm lapping up toot la cava
Iike a braw señora brava
What a bloody great July!
(Where I've put the little 'x'
is where Juan and I had sex.)

DAVID MARK WILLIAMS

Free Cake For All

The cake is free, freer than money
and the meatheads gather to shout
no more, no more
through megaphones for only the birds to hear

but come the day
see us tramping beaches beyond lockdown
in skimpy clothes and lumpy wellingtons
who cares what we look like, eh,
dropping litter, broken rules,

best summer ever should not be allowed
to go by us and the rat population's
through the roof now,
up into the impossible blue
billowed with mackerel clouds.

www.ingramcontent.com/pod-product-compliance
Lightning Source LLC
Chambersburg PA
CBHW020035120526
44588CB00031B/868